D0508073

freestyle
SOCCER STREET MOVES

Acknowledgments

A huge thank you to all the players who gave up their time to show me their favorite moves and especially to those who appear in this book. Without your enthusiasm and talent *Freestyle Soccer Street Moves* never would have happened.

A vital part of this book is the quality of the images, so another huge thank you to April Ward. She really doesn't know anything about soccer, but manages to capture the energy and beauty of the moves in her fantastic photographs as if she were a fanatical supporter.

Lastly, I want to thank my family — Ethel, Romany, Seamus and Saskia — who have to put up with me always talking, watching, breathing and thinking about soccer. Thank you.

freestyle
SOCCER STREET MOVES

tricks   stepovers   passes

FIREFLY BOOKS

A FIREFLY BOOK

Published by Firefly Books Ltd. 2010

Copyright © 2009 Sean D'Arcy

All rights reserved. No part of this publication may be reproduced, stored in a retrieval system, or transmitted in any form or by any means, electronic, mechanical, photocopying, recording or otherwise, without the prior written permission of the Publisher.

First printing

Publisher Cataloging-in-Publication Data (U.S.)
 D'Arcy, Sean.
   Freestyle soccer street moves : tricks, stepovers, passes / Sean D'Arcy.
[128] p. : col. photos. ; cm.
Summary: Instructional guide to soccer tricks including passing the ball to yourself through another player's feet, passing to another player with style, and using fancy moves to run past another player.
ISBN-13: 978-1-55407-583-6 (pbk.)
ISBN-10: 1-55407-583-1 (pbk.)
1. Soccer – Juvenile literature. 2. Soccer. I. Title.
796.334 dc22   GV943.25D373 2010

A CIP record is available for this book from Library and Archives Canada

Cover design by Jocelyn Lucas and James Watson
Text design and typesetting by James Watson
Cover photograph © April Ward
Inside photographs © April Ward, except p 6, courtesy of the author

Published in the United States by
Firefly Books (U.S.) Inc.
P.O. Box 1338, Ellicott Station
Buffalo, New York 14205

Published in Canada by
Firefly Books Ltd.
66 Leek Crescent
Richmond Hill, Ontario L4B 1H1

First published in 2009 by A&C Black Publishers Ltd

Printed and bound in China by South China Printing Co.

Note: It is always the responsibility of the individual to assess his or her own fitness capability before participating in any training activity. While every effort has been made to ensure the content of this book is as technically accurate as possible, neither the author nor the publishers can accept responsibility for any injury or loss sustained as a result of the use of this material.

CONTENTS

Introduction

Hello, my name is Sean D'Arcy and I am a professional soccer freestyler and street soccer player. I am going to show you how to do some world-class street moves that will make you the player everybody else wants to be.

The book is divided into three sections: Nutmegs, Trick Passes and Beat Moves.

Nutmegs are the ultimate in street soccer, when you put the ball through another player's legs and then go past them. Everybody likes doing it, but it isn't much fun when it gets done to you.

Trick Passes are when you are in a tight situation and really need something special to get the ball to another player.

Beat Moves: this is what it's all about. When going past a player isn't enough — you have to go past them with style!

Learning these moves will unleash your creative ability and make it easy for you to express your talent in all types of situations. The best players in the world all started developing their skills playing street soccer, without coaches screaming instructions at them or worrying about what the score was. These players learned how to solve problems on their own and had all the time in the world to practice what moves worked best for them.

For you street soccer players who also love freestyling, I have written a book called *Freestyle Soccer Tricks* that shows you how to do amazing freestyle juggling tricks.

I had a brilliant time writing this book, but if you need any more tips then go to my website (www.footballtricks.com) and I'll be glad to help you out.

Street soccer is about playing with style, confidence and creativity. So don't you think it's time you stopped reading the introduction and started learning the moves?

Nutmegs

There are two sides to every nutmeg. It is brilliant if you are doing it and not so brilliant if it is getting done to you, but that's what makes them so wonderful. All my favorites are in here. I have divided this chapter into two sections: nutmegs when you are facing a defender and nutmegs with your back to them.

Facing the Defender

THE FUSE

This is a real favorite of mine and one that I have loved since the first time I saw it. If I am honest it has been done to me almost as many times as I have done it to others.

Step 1

Start with the ball in front of you, then step over the ball with your left foot.

Step 2

Gently tap the ball forward and to your right with the inside of your right foot.

Secret

The slower you do Steps 1 and 2 then the more likely this nutmeg will work.

Tip

When you do the step over in Step 1 make sure you put your left foot down out of the way so there is enough room for the ball to go right in Step 2.

Step 3

Nutmeg with the outside of your left foot.

Remix

This remix adds that extra style to an already stylish move. In Step 3 stop the ball with the sole of your left foot just for a split second, then roll through the nutmeg while you spin around the defender.

Common Problem

I always hit the closest foot of the defender.

This is because in Step 2 you are only tapping the ball forward and not to the right.

ZOOM ZOOM

I love this nutmeg because the defender knows exactly what you did, but they just couldn't stop it.

Step 1

It is best to start with the ball near your right foot. Tap the ball across in front of your body with the inside of your right foot.

Step 2

Do a little hop to your left and tap the ball back across in front of you with the inside of your left foot.

Tip

You need to make sure that the ball goes far enough in Step 1 to convince the defender that you are going in that direction, so they will open their legs for the nutmeg.

Step 3

Nutmeg with the inside of your right foot.

Remix

This is a very subtle remix, but makes the move look very different. In Step 1 drag the ball across in front of you with the sole of your right foot. This makes you appear to be moving both to your left and your right at the same time, which just leaves the defender bamboozled.

Secret

Do a little hop — just enough to make it look as if you are going to your left.

Common Problem

I always hit the inside of the defender's right foot when I try to nutmeg.

You are missing out the hop to the left in Step 2 so the ball doesn't go far enough to make the defender open their legs for the nutmeg.

BANG BANG

This is an unusual nutmeg because you are not trying to fool the defender, but just move the ball too fast for them.

Step 1

Start with the ball close to the inside of your left foot.

Tip

Speed is essential in Step 1 — you must move the ball quicker than the defender can move their feet.

Step 2

Using the inside of your left foot pass the ball forward and to the right in front of you.

Step 3

Nutmeg through with the inside of your right foot.

Remix

This is the way I prefer to do this nutmeg. At the very start do a step-over with your right foot, but don't put your right foot back down on the ground. Now in Step 2 you hop to pass the ball with the inside of your left foot. The defender is taken by surprise by the hop, which gives you time to do Step 3 before they can react. It makes me smile just thinking about it...

Secret

Start with the ball very close to the inside of your left foot — the defender will have less time to react to you moving.

Common Problem

I always hit the defender's right foot.

With the Bang Bang it's all about moving the ball to a spot where you can do the nutmeg. You are not moving the ball far enough in Step 2 to allow the nutmeg to happen in Step 3.

PUSH-PULL

I fall for this one every time. It is just so tempting to go for the ball since it is so close, but once you do that it's all over.

Step 1

Using the inside of your right foot push the ball forward to the left so that it is very close to the defender's foot.

Tip

In Step 1 the bigger the distance you push the ball, the better.

Step 2

Stop the ball with the sole of your right foot and pull the ball back to where it started.

Step 3

Now nutmeg through with the inside of your right foot.

Remix

I saw this remix done only once and it was just so perfect I have to tell you about it. A player did the Push-Pull at the defender's right foot, but instead of the nutmeg he did it again, this time to the defender's left foot. I think you can guess what happened next — the player managed to get the nutmeg in just before the defender fell flat on their backside.

Common Problem

It never works.

There are two reasons for this: you could be doing it so quickly that the defender has no time to move his foot before you drag the ball back; or you could be stopping the ball so far away that the defender isn't tempted to go for it.

THE "L"

This is the first nutmeg that was ever done to me and I can still remember having absolutely no idea what had happened. Unfortunately, I can also clearly remember my brother laughing behind me as he ran away with the ball.

Step 1

Start with the ball on your right.

Step 2

Gently tap the ball across in front of your body with the inside of your right foot.

Tip
The bigger the distance the ball moves in Step 2, the better.

23

Step 3

Nutmeg through with the outside of your right foot.

Remix

This is a cool remix where you just switch everything around. In Step 2 use the outside of your foot to gently tap the ball to the right, away from your body, and in Step 3 use the inside of your right foot to nutmeg.

Secret

You don't need to be that close to the defender to do this one.

Common Problem

The ball always hits the defender.

You are doing Step 2 too quickly, so the defender has no time to take the step that you need to be able to nutmeg them.

TOP OF THE WORLD

This nutmeg blew me away the first time I saw it and it still does. It's a great move, but it is an ankle-breaker, that's for sure.

Step 1

With both feet jump on top of the ball and balance.

Tip

Make sure you practice balancing on top of the ball on grass so it doesn't hurt so much when you fall. Taking some air out of the ball so it's a bit soft also makes it easier to balance.

Step 2

Jump off and roll the ball to your right using the sole of your right foot.

Step 3

Nutmeg through with the inside of your right foot.

Remix

This remix is very cruel. In Step 1 when you are on top of the ball do a quick twist to the left or right, then back to the middle before you do the nutmeg. This makes the defender twitch big time.

Secret

The secret is all in the timing — you have to wait on top of the ball until the defender tries to kick it away, before you jump off.

Common Problem

I never jump off quick enough.

You have to jump off *the instant* you see the defender begin to move.

THE PUSHER

When The Pusher is done properly the defender knows that a trick is coming, but they just cannot stop it. Brilliant.

Step 1

Push the ball forward and to the left with the inside of your right foot, then stop the ball with the sole of your right foot.

Tip

Don't try to do Step 1 too quickly — remember that this part is just setting the defender up for the nutmeg.

Step 2

Do a little hop off your left foot so that you land next to the ball.

Step 3

Repeat Steps 1 and 2, but this time when you hop don't land next to the ball. Instead, nutmeg through with the inside of your left foot.

Remix

This is a remix that you have to keep for the right occasion since it is so special. Do Steps 1 and 2 the same, but in Step 3 don't hop off your left foot — instead, roll the nutmeg through with the sole of your right foot as you spin around the defender.

Secret

Don't push the ball so close to the defender in Step 1 that they think about tackling for it.

Common Problem

I never get to Step 3.

You are pushing the ball too far in Step 1, which makes the defender open their legs too early and before you are ready. In this move you push the ball twice, so just go half the distance.

Back to the Defender

THE JOHAN

If there is such a thing as a classic street nutmeg, then this is it. Simple, but sweet.

Step 1

Start with the sole of your right foot on top of the ball.

Step 2

Drag the ball back behind your left leg.

Tip

Steps 2 and 3 have to be done very quickly, before the defender has time to react.

Step 3

Nutmeg through with the inside of your right foot.

Remix

For a wonderful remix, in Step 3 instead of hitting the ball with the inside of your right foot, just gently push it forward and stop the ball with the outside of your right foot. When the defender moves, nutmeg through with the toes of your right foot.

Secret

Make sure you have your body in the way and the defender cannot see the ball when you drag it back in Step 2.

Common Problem
I always hit the defender's back foot.

In Step 3 the ball goes forward around the other side of your left leg when you nutmeg. You are hitting the ball sideways, so that's why it hits the back foot.

HOLD'EM HOP

This move has come straight from futsal (indoor soccer with a heavier, low-bounce ball), but is already a firm favorite on the streets.

Step 1

Start with the sole of your right foot on top of the ball.

Step 2

Keep your right foot on top of the ball. Hop off your left foot and spin to face the defender.

Tip

In Step 2 swing your arms around when you do the hop to confuse the defender.

Step 3

Before you land, roll the nutmeg through with the sole of your right foot.

Remix

You could call this a double nutmeg remix. In Step 2, instead of hopping, roll the ball straight at the inside of your left foot. Now step over the ball and let it go though your legs — then nutmeg the defender. A beauty, and very hard to defend against.

Secret

You need some space to do the hop in Step 2, so back into the defender a bit before you hop.

Common Problem

The ball always hits the defender's foot and never goes through cleanly.

What's happening is that in Step 3 you are rolling the ball in the direction you are hopping and not concentrating on it going through the legs.

TWISTER

A sweet nutmeg. It works great if you are running toward the ball with a defender chasing you.

Step 1

Step over the ball with your right foot and plant it down on the other side, with the outside of your right foot closest to the ball.

Step 2

Spin around so you are facing the defender.

Tip

When you step over the ball you have to make it look as if you are going to run away from the defender.

Step 3

Nutmeg through with the outside of your right foot.

Remix

This is a terrific way to change the twister. In Step 1 do a step-over, but put the sole of your right foot on top of the ball. Then spin with your foot still there so you are facing the defender, and simply nutmeg through with the sole of your right foot.

Secret

The nutmeg is a flick rather than a tap, so make sure your foot is close to the ball in Step 1.

Common Problem

The ball always goes up and hits the defender.

In Step 3 you are slicing your foot under the ball and that is what makes it go up. Just spin with your weight a bit more on your heel.

ZIGZAG

This is a fabulous move and a real favorite of a friend of mine. Lucky for me I can guess when he is going to try it, so he hasn't got me yet.

Step 1

With the sole of your right foot roll the ball back toward the inside of your left foot.

Tip

Don't try to do this move too quickly. It will still work even if done slowly; the defender cannot see the ball and the hop will take them by surprise.

Step 2

Very gently hop off your left foot and tap the ball to your right with the inside of your left foot.

Common Problem

I can never do the last bit with the inside of my right foot.

Remember, the hop in Step 2 is just to change the position of the ball and it doesn't have to be done quickly. Just a gentle hop and a tap.

Step 3

Nutmeg through with the inside of your right foot.

Remix

Apart from looking great it is better to use this remix when there is less space behind the defender, as the ball goes through slower. In Step 3, instead of using the inside of your right foot to nutmeg the defender, you use the sole of your foot.

Secret

Keep your right foot in the air the whole time until you have done the nutmeg.

C.U.

This is my favorite nutmeg at the moment. It is called the C.U. because once a friend of mine did this and as the ball went through he shouted "See you" for absolutely no reason. It was just so funny that the name has stuck ever since.

Step 1

Start with the sole of your right foot on top of the ball and hop off your left foot. Spin so that you are now almost facing the defender.

Step 2

Drag the ball with the sole of your right foot toward your left foot.

Tip

The C.U. has to be done quickly, before the defender can react, so do the steps fast.

Step 3

Keeping your left foot in the air the whole time, nutmeg through with the outside of your left foot.

Remix

This is just a wonderful remix that even changes which way you go around the defender. This time in Step 1 take a big hop and allow the ball to roll as far as you can before using the inside of your left foot to nutmeg. You want the defender to react and take a step in the direction the ball is going before you nutmeg.

Secret

Don't try to do a really big hop as it will be difficult to keep your balance.

Common Problem

The defender is always able to get between me and the ball after the nutmeg.

This is because in Step 2 you are only tapping the ball forward and not to the right.

ANNAP

This is the ultimate nutmeg when the ball actually goes back toward you. Just awesome.

Step 1

Using the sole of your right foot roll the ball back toward your left foot, letting it roll past your foot and the defender.

Tip

Don't do it to someone who owes you money, as they will never pay you back after this!

Step 2

Holding the defender off, reach out for the ball and stop it with the sole of your left foot.

Step 3

Spin and nutmeg backward with the sole of your left foot.

Remix

If this is the ultimate nutmeg, how can you expect to have a remix that makes it look better?!

Secret

In Steps 1 and 2 it is vital that the defender cannot see the ball, so you need to make sure your body is in the way.

Common Problem

The defender always bumps me before I do the nutmeg.

Remember that you have to make sure the defender cannot see the ball before you try it.

GLUE FOOT NUTMEG

A joy to watch, and when it's done properly this is just unstoppable.

Step 1

Fake a pass with the inside of your right foot, but only *gently* make contact with the ball.

Tip

Don't try to roll the ball too quickly or it will move off your foot.

Step 2

Using the inside of your right foot, roll the ball in an arc as you spin around to almost face the defender.

Step 3

Continue the arc and nutmeg through with the inside of your right foot.

Remix

This is one of those moves that when defending I just can't stop myself from going for the ball. In Step 2 do a bigger arc with the ball and stop it with the sole of your right foot in front of the defender. As soon as the defender moves, nutmeg through with the sole of your right foot.

Secret

The Glue Foot only works if you've convinced the defender you are going to pass the ball — the fake pass is the secret.

Common Problem

The ball always hits the defender's back foot or sometimes doesn't even go through their legs.

You're pushing the ball too quickly, so you are losing control of the ball just as you try to nutmeg.

Trick Passes

A Trick Pass is when you have to do something extra special to get out of a tight situation. The defender knows you need to pass so you need to disguise where the ball is going. Who is thinking quickest — you or the defender?

THE HENRY

Named after the great Arsenal player and French International, Thierry Henry, who was the first player I ever saw do it in a game. He brought a little bit of street soccer to the English Premier League.

Tip

When you're first learning this trick don't try to hit the ball too hard, as you can easily step on the ball and hurt yourself.

Step 1

Approach the ball as if you were going to hit it with your right foot.

Step 2

As you place your left foot down, hit the ball with the inside of your left foot so the ball goes sideways.

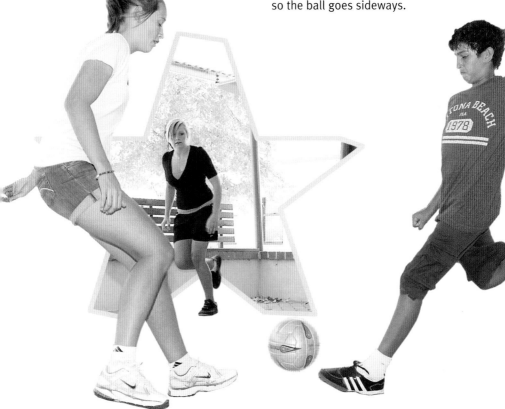

Step 3

Swing through with your right foot, but miss the ball completely.

Remix

In Step 2, instead of hitting the ball with the inside of your left foot, poke it forward with your toes. This remix can be used to take a street penalty kick. Great when they go in, but embarrassing when you poke the ball straight at the goalie.

Secret

In Step 3 swing through with your right foot quite slowly otherwise you might still hit the ball.

Common Problem

I always look really awkward and it works only sometimes.

It's difficult because you feel you are putting your left foot down in the wrong place, but it will be fine if you practice it enough. I imagine I am hitting an invisible ball with my right foot which is next to the real one.

AROUND THE CORNER

This was the first trick pass I ever learned and for some stupid reason I can hit the ball almost twice as far and twice as accurately with my weaker foot.

Step 1

Approach the ball as if you were going to hit a long pass with your left foot.

Tip

To get a more accurate pass use the laces on your right foot. You can use your toes, but the pass will be harder to control.

Step 2

Plant your left foot down with the outside of your foot closest to the ball.

Step 3

Swing your right foot around the back of your left foot and hit the ball with your right foot.

Remix

Do the same move, but this time jump and do a volley with the ball in the air. It looks fantastic and is guaranteed to fool any defender.

Secret

Relax and do the pass slowly. The quicker you do it the more chance the defender has to block it.

Common Problem

I can hardly kick the ball at all and just end up kicking the back of my left leg.

In Step 2 make sure the ball is closer to the outside of your left heel than your toes, so you can hit it without kicking yourself.

"DB"

Jay Jay Okocha, the brilliant Nigerian international, did this astonishing move quite a few times when he played for Bolton in the English Premier League.

Step 1

Take a large step over the ball with your left foot so your foot is planted directly in front of the ball.

Step 2

With the toe of your right foot lift the ball up slightly.

Tip

In Step 2 don't try to scoop the ball up. Lift it so the ball just comes off the ground.

Step 3

Snap back your left foot and pass the ball backward in the air with your left heel.

Remix

This remix is for when you want to pass over a shorter distance. In Step 2 don't lift the ball up — instead, smash the ball into your left heel with the inside of your right foot (closer to the heel). This time the ball just ricochets off your heel behind you.

Secret

In Step 1 your left foot has to be far enough in front to allow the space for your left heel to snap back and generate some power.

Common Problem

The ball gets tangled up between my feet and goes nowhere.

This can happen for two reasons. Firstly, you could be lifting the ball forward in Step 2 and so the ball hits your left calf and not your heel. Or secondly, you're not taking a big enough step over the ball in Step 1.

CANNON

I actually saw a defender pass the ball like this during the World Cup, when two attackers thought they were going to win the ball. Talk about cool under pressure!

Step 1

Start by putting your right foot on top of the ball.

Tip

The farther away the ball is in Step 1, the longer you can hit the pass.

Step 2

Drag the ball back toward the inside of your left foot.

Common Problem

Sometimes the ball goes in the air.

This happens when you drag the ball back too quickly; the ball hits your foot just as you hop and it goes upward.

Step 3

Hop off your left foot and pass the ball with the inside of your left foot.

Remix

This superb remix is for when you are in a really tight space and have to get your pass away quickly. This time, instead of dragging the ball, you back-heel the ball with your right foot toward the inside of your left foot.

Secret

The hop is what generates the power — you don't need to drag the ball back quickly.

HEEL LOB

Just an awesome way to pass the ball when you are tightly marked and don't have any space to move. More than once, I have tried to run in behind a player to pinch the ball and have been hit in the face by this move.

Step 1

Squeeze the ball between your feet.

Common Problem

I never get the ball to go high in the air.

Lift your knee up higher in Step 2 and the ball will go higher, making it easier to back-heel the ball upward.

Step 2

Quickly lift up your right knee so the ball spins up in the air.

Tip

The quicker you lift your right knee the higher the ball goes.

Step 3

Back-heel the ball in the air with your right foot.

Remix

This remix is very difficult to do accurately, but is a game-stopper when it comes off. Do Steps 1 and 2 as normal, but in Step 3 take a big step forward with your right foot and back-heel the ball with your left just after it bounces.

Secret

This trick doesn't have to be done super-fast — just concentrate on going through the steps smoothly.

AIR SWING

There are two things that happen if you do this pass properly — the defender looks bamboozled and you smile. The ball must be coming to you in the air, so you have to choose the right time.

Step 1

As the ball comes to you in the air place your foot down slightly to the left of where the ball will land.

Step 2

Pretend to volley the ball, but swing your right foot over it instead.

Tip
In Step 2 swing really slowly so you don't hit the ball.

Step 3

Allow the ball to bounce off your left foot and go to the right.

Remix

A stunning remix is when you volley the ball over the head of the defender. You need to make sure the defender is far enough away to do this. Do Steps 1 and 2 the same, but in Step 3 hop off your left foot and volley the ball with the laces of your left foot.

Secret

The hardest part of the Air Swing is Step 1, so practice that without doing Step 2 when you are learning the pass.

Common Problem

The ball always goes straight to the defender.

Simple: in Step 1 you are putting your foot down where the ball will land instead of slightly to the left so the ball bounces forward and not to the right.

THE POP

A simple, elegant move that can deceive even the best defenders.

Step 1

Start with the ball in front of your right foot. Shape your body as if you were going to pass the ball to the left with the inside of your right foot.

Step 2
Gently tap the ball across your body
with the inside of your right foot.

Tip
If you are looking to your left in Step 2
it really confuses the defender.

Step 3

Hop off your left foot and hit the ball to the right with the inside of your left foot.

Remix

A stupendous remix! Instead of shaping to pass in Step 1, step forward over the ball with your right foot and spin. Next, gently back-heel the ball with your right foot then hop off your left foot and back-heel with your left. It looks amazing, but remember to gently back-heel the first touch.

Secret

Start with the ball out to the right, the farther the ball travels in Step 2 the harder it is to defend against.

Common Problem

The ball always goes forward and hits the defender.

In Step 2 you are hitting the ball forward as well as across, so in Step 3 the ball hits the toe of your left foot and not the inside of it.

THE ISSY

I can still remember seeing this for the first time and just thinking — I have to learn how to do that!

Step 1

Flick the ball straight up with your right foot to about waist height and slightly out to your right.

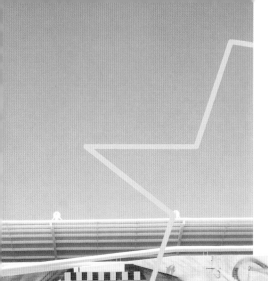

Step 2

Now spin around quite slowly. As you spin put your left leg out behind you to your right, so the ball will land on your left calf.

Tip

Remember to spin slowly until the ball hits your calf.

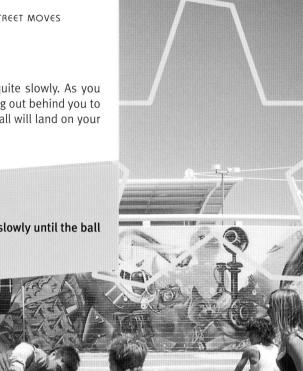

Step 3

Continue your spin and quickly straighten out your left leg. The ball bounces off your calf before hitting your left foot and shooting off.

Remix

This remix requires unbelievable timing, but all the practice is worth it. Do Step 1 the same, but in Step 2 bounce the ball off your backside before you let it land on your calf.

Secret

In Step 1 make sure the flick up isn't too close to your body so you have room to do the trick.

Common Problem

I can never get to Step 3. The ball always drops to the floor off my calf.

Your left leg is already straight when the ball hits, so it doesn't bounce off to hit your left foot.

THE ROLLER

I love this pass although many times I have been hit in the face, and lower if you know what I mean, by players who have not done it properly. It can be a trick shot to use if you are running away from goal.

Step 1

Start with the toes of your right foot on top of the ball which should be straight behind you.

Step 2

Roll the sole of your foot along the top of the ball and downward, until your toes touch the ground.

Step 3

As soon as your toes touch the ground, snap your heel backward to hit the ball up in the air behind you.

Remix

This remix is really a fantastic way to beat a defender and pass to yourself. Do Step 1 the same, but in Step 2 jam your toes into the ground to get the ball to bounce up. Lean forward before quickly snapping your right heel up. The ball will now go over your head and the defender's head, then you run around them, collect the ball and shout "Ole!".

Secret

Don't try to do it too fast. Move smoothly and the ball will travel further.

Tip

Don't try to start the move with the ball too far behind you. Your toes should touch the ground a little way past your left foot.

Common Problem

The ball bangs off my heel and shoots away before I can back-heel it in Step 3.

This is what happens when the ball starts too far behind you in Step 1. The way to check this is to see if your right foot is still behind you when your toe touches the ground.

Beat Moves

These moves are why soccer is called the beautiful game. Every one of them is a crowd-pleaser and it makes you feel good just doing them. Enjoy!

Facing the Defender

ELASTICO

A brilliant move made famous by Ronaldinho, but it was actually used by another famous Brazilian international, Rivelino before Ronaldinho was even born.

Step 1

Start with the ball directly in front of you. Lift your right foot up so it's above your left foot.

Step 2

Brush past the ball with the outside of your right foot so the ball moves slightly to your right.

Tip

Where the ball starts in Step 1 is very important — make sure it's straight in front of you and not over to your right.

Step 3

Now flick the ball to your left with the inside of your right foot and sprint past the defender.

Remix

This move looks good on the ground, but when it is done in the air it defies description! Flick the ball up any way you want, so the ball is straight in front of you, then just do it. No defender can stop the Air Elastico — they can only get lucky.

Secret

Only brush against the ball in Step 2 so the ball barely moves. Don't hit it.

Common Problem

The ball always goes forward and not to my left.

This happens when you hit the ball too hard in Step 2. Remember: just brush against the ball. You could also be trying to do the move too fast.

THE SLAP

The Slap is a favorite of mine and can fool even the best defender. The name comes from the loud slapping noise made when the foot hits the top of the ball.

Step 1

Place your left foot down next to the ball and shape your body as if you were going to pass the ball with the inside of your right foot to the left.

Step 2

Hit the top of the ball with the inside of your right foot and do a little hop to the left off your left foot.

Tip

Don't try to hit the ball too hard in Step 2.

Step 3

Maintain contact with the ball and roll your foot over the top. Plant it down on the other side of the ball so it stops when it hits the outside of your right foot. Now sprint away from the defender in the opposite direction.

Remix

A sneaky remix this one. Do everything the same, but use the toes of your right foot to hit the ball in Step 2. This time the ball rolls over your toes in Step 3 and away from the defender, who isn't sure if you have passed the ball or still got it.

Secret

The most important part of this move is the easiest — in Step 1 you have to convince the defender you are going to pass the ball.

Common Problem

I can do it, but I'm always off balance in Step 3 so I can't sprint away.

This is because you are forgetting the little hop in Step 2. If your legs are crossed before you do Step 3 then this is definitely the problem.

HOCUS POCUS

This is one of those awesome moves that just makes everyone go "Wow!". Surprisingly, I have seen it done many times in pro games, as well as on the street.

Step 1

Start with the ball directly in front of you, now step over the ball with your left foot and plant it on the other side of the ball.

Tip

Don't try to do the trick too fast. It works best when everything is done smoothly.

Step 2

Tap the ball forward and behind your left leg with the inside of your right foot.

Step 3

Now swing your right foot around and tap the ball to the right in front of your left leg with the outside of your right foot. Now sprint past the defender who has no idea where you are going.

Remix

This terrific remix is minimal, but it changes the move altogether. Do all the steps the same, but after Step 3 swing your right foot back around your left leg, and take the ball with the inside of your right foot.

Secret

Just tap the ball in Step 2 — it isn't a big hit.

Common Problem

The ball always goes forward and hits the defender.

This happens when you only tap the ball sideways in Step 2. The ball needs to go forward as well.

RONNY

Done at full pace this move is a thing of beauty and impossible to stop. It has been perfected by Cristiano Ronaldo and no one does it better.

Step 1

While running, use the sole of your right foot to quickly drag the ball forward and across in front of your body.

Tip

Start with the ball as far to the right in Step 1 as is comfortable. The farther the ball moves in Step 1 the more likely the defender is to be tricked.

Step 2

With the inside of your left foot, tap the ball back across in front of your body .

Common Problem
I always lose control of the ball.

This is because players tend to do the whole move quickly, but the only part that needs to be done fast is Step 1. In Step 2 only *tap* the ball so it is easier to keep under control.

Step 3

Step forward with your right foot and allow the ball to roll behind your right leg, then sprint away from your defender to your right.

Remix

A remix that will make even the defender smile, although I'm sure they will try not to show it. In Step 3 tap the ball back again to your left with the inside of your right foot. This time allow the ball to roll behind your left leg.

Secret

After dragging the ball across in Step 1, place your right foot down on the ground so you can step forward with your left foot.

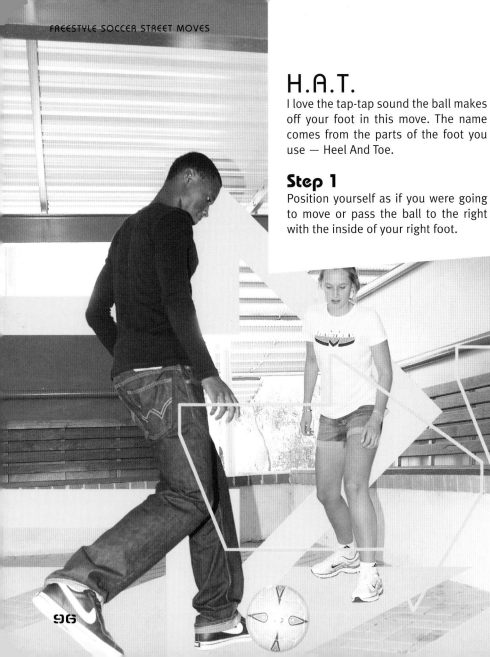

H.A.T.

I love the tap-tap sound the ball makes off your foot in this move. The name comes from the parts of the foot you use — Heel And Toe.

Step 1

Position yourself as if you were going to move or pass the ball to the right with the inside of your right foot.

Step 2

Gently tap the ball to the right with the inside of your right heel.

Tip

That tap-tap sound means you're doing it properly.

Common Problem

I get the sound, but the ball goes forward and not to the left.

You are hitting the ball too hard in Step 2, so your big toe cannot flick around quickly enough in Step 3 to tap the ball and can only deflect it forward.

Step 3

Quickly flick the big toe of your right foot around and tap the ball to the left.

Remix

I saw Cristiano Ronaldo do this awesome remix for Manchester United against Millwall in the FA Cup Final. He did all the steps the same, but he used the outside of his right heel and his little toe to flick the ball. As usual for him, it worked.

Secret

Move your foot very slowly in Step 2 and allow the sound of the ball being hit to trick the defender.

ZORRO

This is a dazzling move, but you need to have some room between you and the defender before you can try it. A definite crowd-pleaser, this should leave the defender stuck to the spot.

Step 1

Using the sole of your right foot drag the ball across in front of you and step over the ball with your left foot.

Step 2

Swing your right foot behind your left leg, and with the outside of your right foot tap the ball back across in front of you.

Tip

The ball does not have to move quickly. The three changes of direction will be what trick the defender, not the speed of the ball.

Step 3

Swing your right foot back again. Now tap the ball back to the left with the inside of your right foot, past the defender who is wishing they'd stayed at home.

Remix

To make this even more spectacular, instead of using the inside of your right foot to tap the ball to the left, use the outside of your left foot. If that doesn't get the crowd on their feet maybe it's time to call a doctor.

Secret

Make sure you drag the ball as slowly as you can in Step 1, otherwise you can lose your balance and control of the ball.

Common Problem

I never go past the defender, but always seem to run sideways from them.

In Step 2 you need to tap the ball back across in front of you instead of just forward. This keeps you running straight at the defender and will make sure you go past them in Step 3.

KNEE DROP

There really isn't any other move on the streets that is like this one. Outstanding when it comes off, but there is nowhere to hide if you mistime Step 2.

Step 1

Drag the ball across your body with the sole of your right foot and do a step-over with the same foot.

Tip

When you do the step-over in Step 1 make sure you go between the ball and your left foot first, before you go around the ball.

Step 2

Stop the ball by dropping your left knee on top of it.

Step 3

Stand up, and at the same time tap the ball to the right behind your right foot with the inside of your left leg. Fly past the defender who is still thinking about why your knee is on the ball.

Remix

Like I said, there is nothing else like this move, but you can turn it into a nutmeg. In Step 3 when you stand up and pretend to go right, tap the ball forward with the instep of your left foot instead. The defender won't see the ball and will follow you, which allows you to nutmeg them.

Secret

Drag the ball very slowly in Step 1, otherwise Step 2 is almost impossible to do.

Common Problem

My knee slips off the ball and whacks into the ground. By the way, that hurts.

In Step 2 don't put your weight on the ball, just go low enough to stop it.

ORIGINAL AKKA

The original and, in my eyes, still the best, with a move that is both uncomplicated and unexpected. I will admit that I fall for this just about every time. I never anticipate the touch of the knee until it's too late and they are past me.

Step 1

Flick the ball up any way you want, to about waist height. The ball must be central and quite close to your body.

Step 2

Cross your right knee over in front of your left knee and tap the ball to the right with the outside of your right knee.

Tip

Flick the ball up any way you want, but make sure it isn't spinning when you do Step 2.

Common Problem

I can never control the ball in Step 3, and sometimes I miss it altogether.

This happens when the ball isn't central in Step 1, so you have to reach for the ball in Step 2, which then makes Step 3 very difficult to do.

Step 3

Lean to your left and while the ball is still in the air tap the ball around the defender with the instep of your right foot. Then run past them on the other side.

Remix

This is a stunner. Do everything the same, but in Step 3 use the outside of your right foot to hit the ball over the defender's head. The only difference is that you need to be a little bit farther away when you start, so that you don't hit the defender in the face.

Secret

Make sure your knees cross over in Step 2 and you will have no problems with balance.

THE TRUNDLE

A long-time favorite of mine — so much so that I have tried to stop doing it as I felt I was becoming very predictable. I still love it though.

Step 1

Start with the ball out to your right and make as if you were going to hit a pass with your right foot. Instead, use the sole of your right foot to drag the ball back behind your left foot.

Step 2

Tap the ball forward around your left foot with the inside of your right foot.

Tip

Just tap the ball in Step 2 so it is easy to stop with the sole of your left foot.

Step 3

Stop the ball with the sole of your left foot and drag it back toward you. Now push the ball to the right, past the defender with the inside of your right foot.

Remix

A beautifully subtle variation is to do everything the same in Steps 1 and 2, but in Step 3 when you drag the ball back with your left foot, do a step-over around the ball. This not only adds some extra style but protects the ball as well.

Secret

The most important part is the fake pass in Step 1. Do that right and the rest will fall into place, as the defender will be off balance.

Common Problem

The defender never falls for it.

You are pushing the ball sideways so the defender doesn't move. Make sure you push the ball forward in Step 2 to make the defender think you are going that way.

"JJ"

The move made famous by the Nigerian player Jay-Jay Okocha. Jay-Jay learned to play on the streets in Nigeria — and what a player he was!

Step 1

With the sole of your right foot, drag the ball forward and across in front of your body.

Tip

The farther you drag the ball in Step 1, the better.

Step 2

Take a big step forward with your left leg
and let the ball roll through your legs.

Step 3

Twist away from the defender and sprint after the ball.

Remix

If you want to be mean you can do the following. When a defender is beaten by a "JJ" they will often spin to chase you, but in the split second that they spin, they cannot see the ball. So, when the defender spins, stop the ball with your left sole and drag the ball back. Go past them on the other side with a big smile on your face!

Secret

Really exaggerate the big step forward in Step 2, as this is what tricks the defender.

Common Problem

The defender falls for the move but still gets the ball.

This is because you are not moving the ball forward in Step 1. If you move it forward as well as across your body, the ball is past the defender before they can react.

OVER & OUT

A cracker of a move, but watch out — I once slipped during the last step and landed flat on my face. There was a big roar from everyone watching and playing, but not the type of roar I was hoping for.

Step 1

Flick the ball up to about waist height.

Tip

Flick it up any way you want, but make sure the ball isn't spinning when it bounces.

Step 2

Jump forward over the top of the ball as it starts to come down.

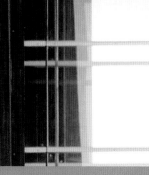

Common Problem

The ball always hits me on the back of my head.

This is because you are arching your back too early, trying to see where the ball is going. You have time to see the ball as you run past the side of the defender, so just lean forward in Step 3.

Step 3

Let the ball bounce up, then smash it down with the instep of your right foot. The ball will now bounce over both your head and the defender's, and you can sprint past the defender on either side.

Remix

This is a superb remix. Do Step 1 the same, but in Step 2 don't jump, just lift your left leg over the ball. When the ball bounces, smash down with the instep of your right, foot sending the ball over the defender's head.

Secret

The higher the ball bounces in Step 3, the better chance you have of getting the ball high enough to beat the defender.

Back to the Defender

TAP TAP

This has everything you want from a street move. The ball changes direction plenty of times and leaves the defender not knowing which way to go, so they end up standing still while you sprint away laughing.

Step 1

Using the sole of your right foot drag the ball across your body.

Step 2

Take a little step to the left and tap the ball back across your body with the inside of your left foot.

Tip
The farther the ball moves in Step 1, the easier it is to trick the defender.

Step 3

Tap the ball back again behind your left leg with the inside of your right foot. Spin away and push the ball past the defender with the inside of your right foot.

Remix

With one little change you can totally alter the look of this move. Do Steps 1 and 2 the same, but in Step 3 drag the ball back with the sole of your right foot and spin to face the defender. Push the ball past them with the inside of your right foot.

Secret

The little step to the left in Step 2 is very important to trick the defender, so try to exaggerate this as much as possible.

Common Problem

I can do it, but the defender always gets the ball off me.

It isn't enough to do the move — you have to *sell* the move. Make sure you start with the ball a long way to the right, then allow the ball to roll a long way to the left before you tap the ball back in Step 2. This will unsettle the defender and you'll trick him.

DOUBLE DUTCH

If you do this quickly enough the defender won't even realize that you have gone past them.

Step 1

Drag the ball back toward you, and tap it with the inside of your right foot and behind your left leg.

Tip

The spin needs to be quick, but Step 1 needs to be done slowly and under control.

Step 2

Spin quickly on your left foot so that you are facing the defender.

Common Problem
The ball always hits the defender.

Remember to only *tap* the ball behind your left leg in Step 1. Don't hit it behind you or you will have to reach for the ball in Step 3, which will cause you to hit the ball into the defender.

Step 3

Tap the ball across your body and past the defender with the inside of your right foot.

Remix

A really fantastic remix is to do Steps 1 and 2 the same, but instead push the ball past the defender with the outside of your left foot in Step 3.

Secret

You can only do this move if you have some room between you and the defender, so don't try it if they are very close.

DRAGS

A cool move that makes the defender think that they are in control. By the time they realize they are not, you will have gone past them.

Step 1

Start with the sole of your right foot on top of the ball and drag it back toward you.

Step 2

Spin on your left foot so that your right shoulder is facing the defender. Stop the ball with the sole of your foot and drag the ball back toward you.

Tip

Don't try this if the defender is really close to you, as you need to have some space to spin and drag the ball.

Common Problem

The defender always manages to bump me off balance when I am spinning.

If the defender is close enough to bump you then you don't have the room to do the Drags move anyway.

Step 3

Spin on your left foot so you are facing the defender and push the ball past them with the inside of your right foot.

Remix

If you have the confidence you can turn this street move into a nutmeg. Steps 1 and 2 are the same, but if the defender has reached out with their foot to poke the ball away, they have left you with a perfect opportunity to nutmeg with the inside of your right foot.

Secret

Drag the ball slowly and far enough back in Step 1 to tempt the defender into making a tackle. By the time they do so, you will have moved the ball again.

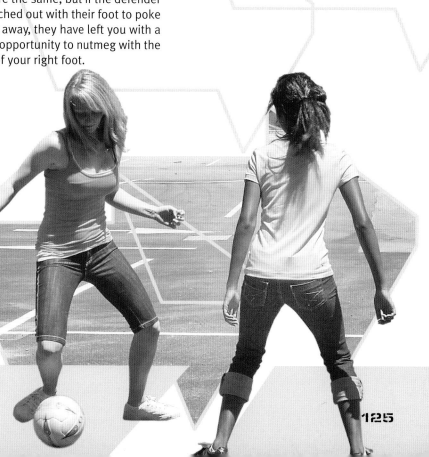

OTT

This is one of those Beat Moves that is quite simply guaranteed to make the defender mad, because it is so simple to prevent if they realize what's happening. Of course, they don't know until it's too late...

Step 1

Flick the ball up any way you want to about waist height.

Step 2

Leave the ball in the air and begin to spin slowly away to your left.

Tip

In Step 1 it is best to flick the ball up in such a way that your body can stay between the ball and the defender. This will make it difficult for them to see the ball.

Step 3

Reach back to the ball with your right leg and back-heel it over the head of the defender. Finish your spin quickly around the defender and get to the ball while the crowd cheers.

Remix

You can turn this superb move into a superb nutmeg, but the defender must fall for your spin in order for it to work. In Step 3 when you reach back for the ball, clamp it to the ground with the sole of your right foot. Then roll the ball back through the defender's legs.

Secret

The higher you lift the ball in Step 1, the easier the move is to do.

Common Problem
The ball alway hits the defender.

In Step 1 make sure when you flick the ball so that it's not spinning in the air. This can make the ball shoot off your heel into the defender.